UBERBITCH

C000282876

The Little Book of
OFFICE
MORONS

Crombie Jardine
PUBLISHING LIMITED

13 Nonsuch Walk, Cheam, Surrey, SM2 7LG
www.crombiejardine.com

Published by Crombie Jardine Publishing Limited
First edition, 2005

ISBN 1-905102-28-3

Sketches by Caitlin Urquhart
Designed by www.glensaville.com
With thanks to CH
Printed & bound in the United Kingdom by
William Clowes Ltd, Beccles, Suffolk

CONTENTS

INTRODUCTION

Office morons... They're all around us, no matter which job or office we find ourselves in, there they are: the Brown-Nosers, Uber-Bitches, Space-Invading Letches, Shit-Shovellers, Wankers, Useless Managers, Jobs-Worths and more.

In this book devoted entirely to office morons, you're guaranteed to recognize someone you know in each category.

UPPER LEVEL MORONS

UPPER LEVEL MORONS

How these people ever got
to the top of the ladder is a
complete mystery. They have
usually been top dog for so long
that they have forgotten what
it was like to be an employee
themselves (presuming they ever
were one in the beginning).

UPPER LEVEL MORONS

Title: Chairman, Managing Director, Senior Director, Company Secretary, Art Director, Marketing Director, Banker, Sales Director, Solicitor, Publishing Director.

Type: Lazy Git, Arrogant Smug Bastard, Filthy Rich One, Wanker.

Names: Hillary, Jeffrey, Randall, James, George, Henry, Jolyon, Orson, Arsen, Diana, Charlotte, Phoebe, Monica, Susannah, Annabelle, Arabella, Patricia, Georgina, Henrietta, Olivia, Zara, Clara, Lara, Jemima.

LAZY GIT

LAZY GIT

OFFICE MOTTO:
A snooze button is a poor
substitute for no alarm
clock at all.

*(Tip: When he asks, "Who's got my
Nuts?" he means the magazine, not
the food, or anything else.)*

LAZY GIT

Why the name?
An annoying, dislikeable, unpleasant, obnoxious or thoughtless person. He has usually been a boss for so long he has forgotten what it means to actually lift a finger himself.

How to identify type
Sits in office with door closed. Uses phone only when obliged. Holds any meetings strictly after 10am and before 11am (so as not to interfere with lunch, or the cricket).

Typical jobs
Chairman or Managing Director.

LAZY GIT

Names
Jeffrey, Jolyon, Michael, George.

Dress code
Old School. Shirts and shoes
from Jermyn Street, suits from
Savile Row. Regimental tie.

Mannerisms
Peering over or round a newspaper, with
a studied expression of slight annoyance
at any interruption; prolonged irritation
if you are an underling who has dared
to space invade. However, if you are
an old school friend, millionaire or
useful contact, LG will bounce out

of leather swivel lean-back chair
and shake hands enthusiastically.

Favourite sayings

- *Dear chap!*
- *Jolly good show!*
- *My dear!*

Meeting Manners

Brief and to the point (particularly
if the meeting is showing signs
of edging towards noon).

Chat-up lines

[Not necessary. Wouldn't know
where to begin anyway. However,
he's very adept at patting female

backsides when squeezing past said females – despite there being enough room to get a tank through.]

Lunches

Not brief and to the point.
Three-hour, boozy ones.

Conversation topics

Abstract subjects: stocks and shares, art… generally anything that makes him feel that he sounds good. No emotional topics whatsoever.

Literature – books and papers

The Times, The Financial Times,
biographies, obscure reports, Old
Boys' Association Newsletter.

Hobbies

Golf. Relaxing at the Club.

Desk and top drawer items

Fountain pen, car keys, photo of
partner and/or kids, a few sheets
of paper, betting slips, membership
card (the local lap-dancing club).

ARROGANT SMUG BASTARD

ARROGANT SMUG BASTARD

> ### OFFICE MOTTO:
> A person who smiles in the
> face of adversity probably
> has a scapegoat.

Why the name?

Feeling or showing proud self-importance and contempt for others, this person usually lives in a totally self-satisfied bubble, utterly unconcerned about the impact he has on everyone else around him.

How to identify type

Talks a lot. Usually very loudly and about self and own (perceived) success. Has an unnatural suntan.

ARROGANT SMUG BASTARD

Typical jobs

Chairman, Senior Director,
Sales Director, Art Director,
Marketing Director, Solicitor.

Names

Randall, Englebert, Henry, Orson,
Egon, Arsen, Alex, Jeffrey, Colin.

Dress code

Still thinks braces (particularly red
ones) are in (think 'Wall Street'). Pin-
striped shirts, waistcoats and suits from
flashy, designer-lead shops. Brylcreem
(and too much). Dyed black hair. Bow
ties. Heel taps. Cufflinks and rings.

Mannerisms

Runs finger up and down nose
(lies a lot), arches one eyebrow,
smirks, runs hand down chest over
stomach in a cat-that's-got-the cream
gesture, runs hands through hair
(because no-one else would).

Favourite sayings

- *My dear girl...*
- *Be a darling.*
- *Run along now.*

Always refers to women as 'ladies' (in a
naturally sleazy, patronizing manner).

Meeting Manners

If he can't lead the meeting or
conversation he sits back in his chair
with a not-terribly-interested-would-
rather-be-lunching-at-The-Ivy look.
Delivers funny-sarcastic quips that more
junior members feel obliged to laugh
at, if nothing other than to relieve
the tension of the inevitable silence.

Chat-up lines

The really cringe-worthy ones,
delivered in the oiliest fashion
possible, with lots of leering and
arching of heavy eyebrows.

ARROGANT SMUG BASTARD

- *If I said you had a wonderful body would you hold it against me?*
- *Did the sun come out or did you just smile at me?*
- *It must be a day off in heaven for an angel like you to be amongst us.*
- *I like every muscle in your body, especially mine.*
- *If it's true that we are what we eat, I could be you by morning!*

Lunches

Long ones, in expensive, showy restaurants with other ASBs or sycophants.

ARROGANT SMUG BASTARD

Conversation topics

The latest sports car or four-wheel-
drive, female or over-the-top-
and-tasteless-but-fantastically-
expensive gadget that is somehow
a nod to the size of ASB's penis.

Literature – books and papers

Purports to read The Financial Times
and The Economist but secretly
subscribes to and avidly reads Nuts and
Front magazines. Reads the 'in' book
of the moment; The Da Vinci Code,
Angela's Ashes, Wild Swans, etc.

ARROGANT SMUG BASTARD

Hobbies

Driving around in latest flash car, trying out the clubs he is too old and untrendy for, in an attempt to impress the ladieez with his wads of cash and bling.

Desk and top drawer items

Feet, newspaper, unopened mail, bottle of whisky for medicinal purposes, condoms, little black book, well-thumbed copy of Fiesta.

FILTHY RICH ONE

OFFICE MOTTO:
The beatings will continue
until morale improves.

Why the name?

Filthy as in dirty or grubby, denoting
the kind of activities or games said
FRO has partaken in to become the
well-heeled lush they are today.

How to identify type

The only form of public transport used is
air travel. Everything else is chauffeur-
driven unless they choose to drive their
own classic car with their car mechanic
in attendance. Always travels first class,
regardless of the length of the journey
and has someone else book the ticket
and arrange their travel to and from
the appropriate destination. Would not

be able to hazard a guess at the rough cost of a pint of milk or a loaf of bread. Has no idea whatsoever what people in his/her employ are paid but suspects it is far too much for their own good.

Typical jobs

Chairman, Managing Director, Publishing Director, Investor, Banker.

Names

Hillary, Humphrey, Jolyon, James, George, Horace, Georgina, Henrietta, Olivia, Zara, Clara, Lara.

Dress code

The most expensive, tailored items from
top-notch shops, the family tailor or
a Savile Row one. Saks, Fifth Avenue.
Muted colours of creams, camels and
navy, with occasional splashes of colour
in ties, scarves, socks or suit linings.
Solid and occasionally flamboyant
shoes. Cufflinks for the men, pearls
and large solitaires for the ladies.

Mannerisms

Impatient tics indicating very
low boredom threshold has been
crossed. Elegant crossing of legs
followed by a straightening of the

trouser crease and removal of non-
existent lint (casual flick of wrist).

Favourite sayings

There are so few people they deign
to speak to, any phrases reported
here would be sheer guesswork.

Meeting Manners

Will only attend the AGM or equivalent.
Expects to be waited upon with five-
star service in everything and will not
tolerate inconsequential calamities.
Anyone unfortunate enough to have
caused the said calamity is expected to
deal with it immediately and eliminate

all trace of it within seconds so as to not affect the sensibilities of the FRO.

Chat-up lines

They wouldn't actually deliver chat-up lines (wouldn't have a clue where to start: the money does the talking). If they wanted to give an indication of interest they would send over a bottle of Champagne (usually accompanied by their card with room number on the back – if the recipient is in luck). They usually sit back and wait to be chatted up.

Lunches

Dinners... breakfasts... every meal... a mystery. But never eats alone.

Always takes three hours. In the company of other FROs only.

Conversation topics

Only talks to other FROs or the current object of desire. Stocks and shares. Sex life.

Literature – books and papers

Nothing remotely funny.

Hobbies

Golf. Tennis. The Club. Classic cars. Making even more money.

Desk and top drawer items

Mont Blanc pen, car keys,
newspaper, freshly opened
mail, a rolodex, a Rollex.

WANKER

WANKER

OFFICE MOTTO:
Teamwork means never
having to take all the
blame yourself.

WANKER

Why the name?
Person who finds pleasure in themselves
as no-one else in their right minds
would even try bothering to get close.

How to identify type
Self-satisfied, totally and utterly ruthless,
would sell their own grandmother
to get what they want. Underhand,
insincere, devious and treacherous.

Typical jobs
Senior Director.

Names
Dan, Donald, Paul, Jeffrey,
Michael, Colin, Lesley.

Dress code

Boring as sin. No dress sense. Austin
Reed for special occasion outfits.

Mannerisms

Sly sliding of the eyes, keeping
the head totally still.

Favourite sayings

- *Oh, I agree with you.*
- *Super.*
- *Absolutely.*

(All false.)

Meeting Manners

Appearing to agree with almost
everyone, but putting in the oar

ever so sweetly whenever possible.
Or suddenly turning the screw and
catching someone totally off-guard and
in a bad light, as they are too stunned
to comprehend what has prompted
such a vicious-but-to-all-intents-and-
purposes-company-interested-and-
completely-impersonal attack.

Chat-up lines

Something fatuous.

- *Just wondering, what would you like
  for breakfast tomorrow morning?*
- *Is that a ladder in your tights? Or
  is it the stairway to heaven?*

- *If I said you had a good body, would you hold it against me?*
- *I wish you were a door so I could bang you all day long.*
- *Get your coat, you've pulled.*
- *I suppose a shag's out of the question?*

Lunches

Out to lunch every day. Always alcohol involved. Will not go to lunch alone; will always do the inviting (as no-one will instigate). Usually

gets someone when that someone
has run out of excuses not to go.

Conversation topics
Other people. And other people's
failures (or investigating ways in which
said failures can be achieved/exploited).

Literature – books and papers
The Times, trade literature.

Hobbies
Wanking, drinking (to relieve the
loneliness or sheer monotony of living),
watching Bad Girls on TV (whilst
imagining self as ruthless prison warder).

WANKER

Desk and top drawer items

Tissues, magazines, selection of carefully-hidden porn magazines.

Whether you are a student looking for your first summer job or a long-time veteran looking for a change of pace, this WANKERS' JOB APPLICATION JARGON should help you avoid landing that job with the moronic wanker boss...

COMPETITIVE SALARY = We remain competitive by paying less than our competitors.

FLEXIBLE HOURS = Work 55 hours, get paid for 37.5.

GOOD COMMUNICATION SKILLS = Management communicates, you listen, then figure out what they want you to do.

ABILITY TO HANDLE A HEAVY WORKLOAD: You whine, you're fired.

SELF-MOTIVATED: Management won't answer questions.

SOME OVERTIME REQUIRED:
Some time each night and
some time each weekend.

DUTIES WILL VARY: Anyone in
the office can boss you around.

COMPETITIVE ENVIRONMENT:
We have a lot of turnover.

**SEEKING CANDIDATES WITH A
WIDE VARIETY OF
EXPERIENCE**: You'll
need it to replace
three people
who just left.

MIDDLE LEVEL MORONS

Well. These people are no longer on the bottom rung of the ladder and feel quite smug about it. Not too smug, as they still have a way to go and still have superiors they must account to. They are often quick to take the credit for work that is either a team effort or nothing to do with them at all, whilst also very

MIDDLE LEVEL MORONS

adept at blaming other lesser mortals for their own negligence or uselessness.

Title: Manager, Line Manager, Supervisor, Executive, Controller, PA, Editor, Officer, Accountant, HR Manager, Lawyer, Trader, Sales Manager, Stock Supervisor.

Type: Romeo, Brown-Noser, Useless Manager, Space-Invading Letch, Hot-Shot, Uber-Bitch, Water-Cooler Philosopher.

Names: Dave, Darren, Michael, Alex, Max, Marco, Omar, Cary, Kyle, Matthew, Mark, Luke and John, Isaac, Jesus, Kyle,

MIDDLE LEVEL MORONS

Stefan, Richard, Melville, Neville, Jay,
Ben, Nicholas, Timothy, Robert, Joe,
Peter, Leslie, Elvis, Chris, Oliver, Patrick,
Ruth, Rebecca, Mary, Philippa, Joanne,
Lesley, Barbara, Davina, Elizabeth,
Janet, Shanice, Monnae, Tina, Tanya,
Tonia, Sonia, Chantelle, Silvia, Tammy,
Uma, Ursula, Mimi, Izzie, Lizzie.

ROMEO

ROMEO

OFFICE MOTTO:
Succeed in spite
of management.

ROMEO

Why the name?

He desperately wants to be loved-up but only whilst it's exciting and heady, sexy and slightly tragic.

How to identify type

Constantly roaming eyes, in the up and down manner.

Typical jobs

Trader or Sales Manager (where he can be out and about), casting net wide and hauling in a varied catch.

ROMEO

Names

Alex, Omar, Cary, Henry, Harvey, Luigi, Giorgio, Mario, Romano, Stefano, Marco, Roberto, Julio, Aristotle.

Dress code

Well-dressed in a designer-smart-casual way, seeking the it's-just-something-I-threw-on-this-morning-I-can't-help-it-if-I'm-gorgeous look. Cargo pants (= trendy).

Mannerisms

Soul-searching looks, designed to make the recipient melt and feel like they are the only one on the room.

Favourite sayings

- *"Aaaah, [name of other person]! [arms outstretched]"* delivered with an exaggerated sigh, and the implication, I've met my true love at last, having roamed the earth for all these years, here you are...

Meeting Manners

Seeks out the eyes of any pretty female in the meeting and plays silent games with her throughout the meeting. If no females are in the meeting it will be the secretary who comes in with the coffee tray.

ROMEO

Chat-up lines

- *What beautiful eyes you have. I feel that I am drowning in them.*
- *I think I must be dying because I'm looking at Heaven.*
- *Is there an airport nearby or is that my heart taking off?*
- *If you were a tear in my eye I would not cry for fear of losing you.*
- *Save me! I'm drowning in a sea of love.*
- *We could make beautiful music together.*
- *What winks and is great in bed? (Wink)*

Lunches

Always buying. At that lovely little bistro where he always manages to get the table in the corner just right for two and seems on brotherly-winking terms with the waiters and owner.

Conversation topics

You. You wonderful, heavenly creature.

Literature – books and papers

Poetry, the classics.

Hobbies

Opera singing (amateurishly, usually to Caruso), cooking pasta, running (away), looking in the mirror.

Desk and top drawer items

Aftershave, mints, condoms, photos,
Jo Malone aftershave, two little
black books, breath fresheners,
spare pair of boxers, hair gel and
comb, overnight essentials.

BROWN-NOSER

OFFICE MOTTO:
Indecision is the key
to flexibility.

BROWN-NOSER

Why the name?

Sniffs out the person who's going to help them achieve and will suck up to them unashamedly arse-kissing all the way. Will probably actually *ask* for an appraisal, on the grounds that this shows initiative (and will obscure general inefficiencies and inadequacies).

How to identify type

Lots of kow-towing, hand-wringing, hands in pocket stance, fidgeting, head slants, rounded shoulders (owing to the weight of the shit collected), slightly sour expression (trying to get rid of the taste in their mouths).

BROWN-NOSER

Typical jobs

Line Manager, Officer, Executive,
Stock Supervisor, HR Manager.

Names

Dave, Darren, Michael, Stefan,
Richard, Melville, Neville, Phillippa,
Lesley, Silvia, Mimi, Izzie, Lizzie,
Steve, Samantha, Clare.

Dress code

Self-effacing, regulation style, heritage
colours. Overall shabby look (but
not of the elegant variety). Shops
in all the places the person above

them in the pecking order has ever recommended or expressed a liking for.

Mannerisms

Forlock tugging, eager-puppy-with-tongue-hanging-out-take-me-for-a-walk expression, nose picking.

Favourite sayings

- *Oh, yes.*
- *That's right.*
- *Of course.*
- *Absolutely.*
- *Super.*
- *Obviously.*
- *Is there anything else I can help you with?*

Meeting Manners

Cringe-worthy to the extreme, not
seeming to have any self-respect as
they fawn all over the superior power
that is. If they feel that the meeting
is an important one then there'll be
lots of note-taking (head bowed,
shoulders hunched, furious scribbling
with tongue out). If the meeting
is deemed unimportant, there'll
be no note-taking whatsoever.

Chat-up lines

If there are any, they are straight
out of a book, with no thought
whatsoever in the delivery.

- *If I could rearrange the alphabet,*
  I'd put U and I together.

More likely to be:

- *Didn't you go to my school?*
- *Is this seat taken?*
- *May I introduce myself?*

Lunches

Arranges to have lunch on a regular (but respectfully infrequent) basis with boss, always planning well in advance, using a work pretext and always ensuring the boss knows that BN will be paying, out of thanks and respect for being allowed to slave away in the shadow of the

Almighty. After lunch will let everyone else know that s/he (the BN) paid.

Conversation topics
Anything and everything their superior would like to talk about.

Literature – books and papers
Anything and everything their superior would like to read about.

Hobbies
Anything and everything their superior would like to do.

Desk and top drawer items
Note pad filled with details of all the boss's favourite drinks, food,

BROWN-NOSER

past times, holiday destination, and birthday, plus detrimental comments certain colleagues have made about top management. Small, inexpensive gifts, and a selection of greetings cards that can be used for most occasions.

USELESS MANAGER

OFFICE MOTTO:
If at first you don't
succeed, try management.

Why the name?

A waste of skin. Useless, as in not able to be used, unsuccessful or unlikely to be worthwhile, not able to do something properly. How they ever got to managerial level is one of life's imponderables.

How to identify type

Buries head in the sand at every given opportunity; the bigger the problem, the deeper the burial. Maintains a rigid silence when there is a bad atmosphere in the office (normally due to said UM's rigid silence). Is happy and chatty and light-hearted if thinks everyone else is happy and chatty and light-hearted. Very susceptible to other people's moods.

Typical jobs

Manager, Line Manager, Supervisor.

Names

Phil, Deborah, Mike, Susan, Rupert, Nigel, George, Lesley, Martin, Kevin, Trevor, Keith, Dave, Barbara, Frank, Eric, Clare, Colin.

Dress code

Slightly off-the-wall number from the local boutique, dark and sombre in colour but unusual in style, accompanied by big and unusual jewellery and accessories. Austin Reed suits for the odd occasion.

Mannerisms

Feigned attentive stance (head to one side), nodding in agreement, eye contact only if interested, otherwise stares into the distance.

Favourite sayings

- *What do you think?*
  [*Not that any notice will be taken of what you think!*]
- *Oh how lovely!*

Meeting manners

Makes a point of appearing objective (which usually means not saying anything) but in reality is thinking only of his/her own position and how to protect this. Will not speak up for or support anyone else, just in case it implicates him/her in some obscure way.

Chat-up lines

Bad ones...

- *Is it hot in here or is it just you?*
- *What time do you have to be back in heaven?*

• *What do you do when you're not being gorgeous?*

Lunches
Frequent. Gossip-laden. Expects everyone to pay their own way (even when the lunch is legitimately for business).

Conversation topics
Restaurants, food, recipes, books, shopping, arty films and plays. Anything that cannot in any way be used against her/him in work.

Literature – books and papers
Historical novels, psychological
thrillers, the classics, Sporting Life.

Hobbies
Gossiping. Cooking and shopping.

Desk and top drawer items
Unopened mail that will eventually
be handed on to an assistant
who will then be blamed for the
delay. Scraps of screwed up paper,
reports, print-outs, chewing gum
wrappers, paperbacks, binoculars.

HOT-SHOT OFFICE MOTTO:
Go the extra mile. It makes
your boss look like an
incompetent slacker.

Why the name?

As fast as a fired bullet, tearing
through the air at the speed of light,
charming every attractive member
of the opposite sex on the way
and outshining everyone else.

How to identify type

Well dressed, well spoken, alert, healthy-
looking, quite loud, extroverted,
humorous, quick-witted, ambitious,
always has a slightly-on-guard look.

Typical jobs

HR Manager, Editor (Commissioning),
Trade, Sales Manager, Banker, Lawyer.

Names
Dorian, Amanda, Davina, Nicholas, Alex, Max, Stefan, Jay, Ben.

Dress code
Flashy, sharp suits (= "Watch this space, I'm going places.")

Mannerisms
Name dropping, always appearing to be on the move (so many important things to do and people to see, so little time).

Favourite sayings
- *Cool.*
- *Fabbo!*
- *Right on!*

Meeting Manners

Quick-witted, concise and to the point.
Pleasant but not friendly. Positive
but not gushing. Great at buttery
delegation. Always manages to avoid
having any work assigned to them.

Chat-up lines

Delivers the old-fashioned lines
with irresistible panache.

- *You with all those curves,
  and me with no brakes.*
- *Are you tired? Because you've been
  running through my mind all day.*

- *Do you believe in love at first sight, or should I walk by again?*
- *I'm a stud muffin baby, why don't you take a bite?*
- *You are so hot, it's people like you that are the real reason for global warming.*
- *Who stole the stars from the sky and put them in your eyes?*

Lunches

Long but not-too-boozy business PR ones.

Conversation topics

Their latest car or holiday.

Literature – books and papers
The Economist, The Financial Times, and Nuts if a man, Vogue if a woman.

Hobbies
Golf for the man (for the social climbing), health spas or retreats for the woman.

Desk and top drawer items
Neatly organized stationery, clear desk, rolodex, Wisden's Almanack, Harden's Restaurant Guide.

SPACE-INVADING LETCH

OFFICE MOTTO:
When the going gets tough, the
tough take a coffee break.

Why the name?

Someone who has no respect for other people's personal space and who behaves lewdly and lustfully towards attractive members of the opposite sex in a way that the latter regard as totally disgusting and distasteful.

How to identify type

Usually has too much scent (to mask the odour problem), a strange haircut, a pallid and slightly sweaty face with hair growing in the wrong places.

Typical jobs

Executive, Controller, Officer, Accountant.

SPACE-INVADING LETCH

Names

Kevin, Nigel, Bill, Will, Phil, Bob,
Rob, Knob, Richard, Wayne,
Dwayne, Shane, Jimmy.

Dress code

Favours brown suits and synthetic
patterned shirts. Formerly had
the title Man at C&A. Now shops
in Matalan, TK Maxx, Burtons.

Mannerisms

Ball-scratching, nose-picking, invading
personal space, leaning in, edging closer.
Innuendo-laden facial expressions.

Favourite sayings
• *While you're down there...*

Meeting Manners
Sits at the table studying all the members of the opposite sex in the room, fantasizing about them being naked and covered in whipped cream.

Chat-up lines
• *Nice legs... What time do they open?*
• *Do you sleep on your stomach... Can I?*
• *If I could see you naked, I'd die happily.*
• *Show us your tits, girl.*

- *Excuse me, I'm new around here. Would you please direct me to your bedroom?*
- *I've got a condom with your name on it.*
- *Why don't you come here and sit on my lap and we'll talk about the first thing that pops up?*
- *While you're down there...*

Lunches

An hour in the local seedy hotel with a prostitute or anyone willing.

Conversation topics

"Did you see Sex Tips for Girls on TV last night?"

Literature – books and papers

Playboy. Titbits. (Nuts for the more educated of the species.)

Hobbies

Wanking and watching porn. Spending time in the lingerie department of Marks & Spencer. Peering down female colleagues' blouses and imagining all sorts of things…

Desk and top drawer items

Weird screen-saver that will hopefully invite comment, free novelty gifts from the trade, overpowering aftershave.

UBER-BITCH

UBER-BITCH

OFFICE MOTTO:
Never underestimate the
power of very stupid people
in large groups.

UBER-BITCH

Why the name?

A merciless, aggressive person
who browbeats others and fills
them with feelings of fear and
inadequacy over a period of time.

How to identify type

Dark fitted suits, stern look, angular
glasses (to peer over), clipped
way of walking and talking.

Typical jobs

Office Manager, Line Manager,
Supervisor, Executive, PA, HR Manager.

Names

Leandra, Philippa, Lesley, Leonora,
Frances, Diana, Sophia, Clara,
Zara, Clarissa, Annabella, Isabella,
Gabriella, Eloisa, Araminta, Clare.

Dress code

Overbearing, Supernanny-style from
Harrods, Jaeger, Hobbs, Harvey Nicks.

Mannerisms

Arched eyebrow (indicating a variety of
emotions), peering over the top of half-
glasses (usually held on chain around
neck when not being peered over).

Favourite sayings

- *Daaaarlinnngh!*
- *You angel!*
- *You look a millions dollars!*
- *Where did you get that...?*

Meeting manners

Assertive, aggressive, wily, patronising.

Chat-up lines

Not shy...

- *Do you work for the post office? I thought I saw you checking out my package.*
- *Would you like an Australian kiss? It's like a French kiss, but down under.*

- *You, me, whipped cream and handcuffs. Any questions?*
- *Can you give me a hand?*
- *I'll show you mine, if you show me yours.*
- *I can read you like a book. I bet you're great between the covers.*

Lunches

Long. Champagne and gossip. Food negligible; perhaps a lettuce leaf pushed around a plate or a stick of celery (but usually only in the Bloody Mary aperitif).

Conversation topics

Anything gossip-worthy.

Literature – books and papers
Tatler, Hello! and OK! magazines.

Hobbies
Shopping, gossiping, drinking,
shopping, gossiping, drinking...

Desk and top drawer items
Dangerously
sharpened pencils,
mobile phone,
feminist literature,
print-outs, projects
and reports.

WATER-COOLER PHILOSOPHER

OFFICE MOTTO:
We waste time so you
don't have to.

Why the name?

A dreamer who seeks to understand and explain the nature of life, who is given to thinking deeply and seriously about human affairs, and who believes the answers are to be found if they can shirk work long enough and hang around the office water cooler engaging in conversation with anyone who happens to pass by.

How to identify type

Looks like they have life's imponderables weighing them down.

Typical jobs
Executive, Controller, PA, Editor, Officer.

Names
John, Jane, Peter, Janet, Jo, Ruth,
Stephen, Michael, David, Corinne, Karl,
Christopher, Timothy, Thomas, Richard,
Matthew, Mark, Luke and John, Isaac,
Jesus, Alison, Toby, Lindsay, Iain.

Dress code
Soft fabrics, heritage colours, loafers,
nubuck, linen and cotton mixes.

Mannerisms
Slow-motion movements accompanied
by an almost tangible expression

of expecting to be disappointed in everything and everyone.

Favourite sayings

- *Do you believe in [...]?*
- *It wasn't meant to be.*
- *What did you make of Corrie / Eastenders last night, then?*

Meeting Manners

See Mannerisms.

Chat-up lines

- *Do your legs hurt from running through my dreams all night?*
- *I think you're the light at the end of my tunnel.*

- *I didn't believe in angels until I met you!*

Lunches
In the summer: a sandwich eaten whilst sitting on a park bench enjoying nature. In the winter: a book in the desk in the office.

Conversation topics
God, your God, the universe, etc.

Literature – books and papers
Anything philosophical, theological or spiritual. Thinkers' World. The Alchemist.

Hobbies
Fly fishing, day dreaming.

Desk and top drawer items

The Big Issue,
Thinkers' Weekly,
an empty glass,
Schott's Miscellany,
Whitaker's
Almanack.

LOWER LEVEL MORONS

Last in the pecking order,
this lot is left to fight it out
amongst themselves, usually
grumbling about it all the way.

LOWER LEVEL MORONS

Title: Assistant, Secretary, Administrator, Office Junior, Post-Room Assistant, Receptionist, Stationery Buyer.

Type: Whinger, Jobs-Worth, Shit-Shoveller, Wimp, Bimbo, Gossiper.

Names: Wayne, Shane, Dwayne, Arnold, Phil, Bill, Stephen, Ian, Paul, Ken, Alan, Ed, Ted, Fred, Barry, Gary, Larry, Harry, Jerry, Sharon, Michelle, Colleen, Tracy, Stacey, Collette, Oprah, Kylie, Cindy, Britney, Daniella, Barbie, Trisha, Norman, Neville, Nigel, Kevin, Trevor, Vera, Mavis, Doris, Ange, Daisy, Maisy, Dolly, Molly, Polly.

WHINGER

WHINGER

OFFICE MOTTO:
Eagles may soar, but
weasels don't get sucked
into jet engines.

WHINGER

Why the name?

To whinge or to moan... to
complain annoyingly, unreasonably,
needlessly and/or continuously about
something that in all probability
is relatively trivial or unimportant
to 99.7% of the population.

How to identify type

Whingers tend to sit hunched over their
keyboards, muttering to themselves,
or talking in subdued tones on the
phone (to some other moaner).

Typical jobs
Secretary, Office Junior, Post-Room Assistant, Receptionist.

Names
Vera, Mavis, Doris, Ange, Nelly, Rodney, Patrick, Richard, Ian, Tina, Tanya, Tonia, Sonia, Chantelle, Melville, Neville, Leslie.

Dress code
Stiff, boring, up-tight golf-wear, nylon, tan tights, pressed trousers, v-necks, patterns (from Littlewoods, Primark, Peacocks, etc.).

Mannerisms

Rolling eyes, pursed lips, variant sighs (ranging from a whiff of exhaling breath to the deepest, darkest ocean of despair).

Favourite sayings

- *For goodness' sake.*
- *I'm so under-valued.*
- *Yeah, right.*
- *I'm just so not having this.*
- *It's not fair. Why me?*
- *Really?*
- *Are you sure?*

- *No?!*
- *Is it me, or...?*
- *As if I would!*
- *Honestly.*

Meeting Manners
N/a – never makes it there.

Chat-up lines
- *Do you have to come here often?*

Lunches
Sandwich at desk.

Conversation topics
Me, me, me. Whinge, whinge, whinge. Launderette prices, rip-

off market merchants, TV soaps,
the sorry state of their finances.

Literature – books and papers
The Daily Mail. Said they'd read a
book once but didn't like it (Jeffrey
Archer). Trashy magazines.

Hobbies
TV watching. Computer games.

Desk and top drawer items
Stupid stickers on computer. Very
tidy desk. Large multi-layered in-tray.
Fluffy toy, picture of them on holiday
with a Saddam Hussein lookalike.

JOBS-WORTH

OFFICE MOTTO:
Doing a job right the first time gets the job done. Doing the job wrong fourteen times gives you job security.

JOBS-WORTH

Why the name?

Jobs-Worth… carrying out duties
or activities that fall strictly within
the remit of a given paid job or
occupation, exercising physical or
mental effort only if salaried to do so.

How to identify type

A belligerent expression, worn with
pride. They're the ones sitting on their
arses surrounded by general chaos:
phones ringing, colleagues rushing
here and there, the photocopier
broken, printers on the blink…

JOBS-WORTH

Typical jobs
Secretary, Office Junior, Post-Room Assistant, Filing Clerk, Stock Control Assistant, Clerical Assistant, Receptionist.

Names
Janet, John, Jeff, Jack, Trevor, Kevin, Jay, Ben, Nicholas, Timothy, Peter, Chris, Ian, Brian, Patrick, Tina, Mimi, Izzie, Lizzie, Nigel, Norman, Philip, Mark.

Dress code
Non-descript but clean, ironed clothes. Any clothes.

Mannerisms

All mannerisms ooze an economy
of movement and a condescending
air. They are masters of the 'Why-
are-you-bothering-me?' look.

Favourite sayings

• *And your point is?*
• *I don't believe that's in my contract.*

Meeting Manners

Will bring in the coffees and teas after
the meeting has started – to make
a point of interrupting you, as you
have interrupted them– delivering
them with a pinched smile.

Chat-up lines

- *Hey, I lost my phone number...
  Can I have yours?*
- *Why don't you come here and sit
  on my lap and we will talk about
  the first thing that pops up.*
- *Fuck me if I'm wrong, but
  don't you want to kiss me?*

Lunches

Sandwiches at desk (bought from the
mobile sandwich company they have
arranged to do the rounds), then an
hour's lunch break off the premises.

Conversation topics

Me, me, me.

Literature – books and papers

The Daily Mail, Heat.

Hobbies

TV watching. Taking sickies when the boss is on holiday. Using the office time to surf the net for another job.

Desk and top drawer items

The Ultimate Book of Sudoku 1, newspaper.

SHIT-SHOVELLER

SHIT-SHOVELLER

OFFICE MOTTO:
If you can stay calm while
all around you is chaos...
then you probably haven't
completely understood the
seriousness of the situation.

SHIT-SHOVELLER

Why the name?
Shit-Shoveller… someone given to lifting, moving or clearing amounts of malodorous or offensive waste material from one place to another.

How to identify type
Permanent stoop from shovelling. A flaring-nostrils thing going on; a conditioning reaction to all the shit being shovelled.

Typical jobs
Assistant.

Names

Nigel, Neville, Norman, Mark,
Catherine, Judy, Julie, Melville, Ben,
Nicholas, Joe, Peter, Chris, Oliver,
Patrick, Ruth, Rebecca, Mary, Colin.

Dress code

Casual, dark colours, self-effacing
outfits – why bother with anything
else? – crumpled suits.

Mannerisms

The occasional forlorn look upwards and
over the spectacles in a kind of tell-me-
you've-come-to-get-me-out-of-here way.

SHIT-SHOVELLER

Favourite sayings

- *Oh... OK.*
- *Never mind.*
- *I'll do that in a minute.*

Meeting Manners

Minute-taking.

Chat-up lines

Shit-Shovellers have no time for chatting up people!

Lunches

What the hell is a lunch?

Conversation topics

No time for chit-chat.

Literature – books and papers

Self-help publications. These tend to remain in the bag as the average SS is so exhausted at the end of the day they hardly have the energy to get ready for bed, let alone read how to do anything else more complicated. Humour – usually black. Travel guides – a form of escapism.

Hobbies

TV watching. Day dreaming.

Desk and top drawer items

Pens, pencils, notepads, calendar, desk diary, holiday brochures.

OFFICE MOTTO:
Aim Low, Reach Your Goals,
Avoid Disappointment.

WIMP

Why the name?

Wimp… Someone failing to try, do or finish something out of fear, a weakness of character and/ or determination or generally a complete absence of backbone.

How to identify type

Self-effacing, weasel-like appearance. The one with the repetitive strain injury, slouched posture and hard-done-by expression.

Typical jobs

Stationery Buyer, Stock Controller, Post-Room Clerk.

WIMP

Names
Kevin, Nigel, Paul, Thomas, Trevor,
Norman, John, Jane, Judith, Colin.

Dress code
Non-descript, unassuming
shades of beige and grey.

Mannerisms
Has a sort of slinky-
shuffling-gliding walk.

Favourite sayings
- *Well...*
- *Um...*
- *Er.*
- *Sure.*

Meeting Manners
N/a.

Chat-up lines
Would be too scared to chat up anyone.

Lunches
Snack/sandwiches at desk.

Conversation topics
Whatever you'd like to talk about.

Literature – books and papers
Geeky subscriptions to
computer magazines, etc.

Hobbies
TV watching. Computer games.

WIMP

Desk and top drawer items

Nothing of any note (except, perhaps, a pot of Vaseline).

OFFICE MOTTO:
Artificial Intelligence is no
match for Natural Stupidity.

BIMBO

Why the name?
Bimbo... Someone lacking in common sense, showing no apparent purpose or rational cause for existence.

How to identify type
Walks around with a dazed, stunned or helpless look on face. But a happy one.

Typical jobs
Office Junior, Secretary, Receptionist.

Names
Stephanie, Kylie, Tina, Tanya, Sonia, Chantelle, Silvia, Tammy, Uma, Ursula, Mimi, Izzie, Lizzie, Clare.

BIMBO

Dress code

Tight short skirts, boobs squashed together and spilling out of top, high heels (= "Hello, Boys"), lots of colour. Top Shop, Primark, Peacocks, Mark One, New Look.

Mannerisms

Wiggling, high-pitched giggling, lots of hair flicking or fiddling, coy sideways glances, eyelash fluttering, etc.

Favourite sayings

- *Oh he never!*
- *I had eight Bacardi Breezers and I never felt a thing!*

BIMBO

- *He only felt my tits within the first half an hour!*

Meeting Manners

N/a.

Chat-up lines

Rarely needs chat-up lines as gives off so many vibes anyone of the opposite sex would see 'available, just come over' written on her forehead. If she were to use lines, they'd be from the school of:

- *Do you believe in love at first sight, or should I walk by again?*

Lunches

Sandwiches and Diet Coke at desk, with a copy of Hello! or something similar for company.

Conversation topics

Men, men and men. TV, hairstyles, makeup, clothes, the minutiae of other people's lives.

Literature – books and papers

Glossy magazines, romance novels.

Hobbies

TV watching, gossiping, going to the beauty salon.

Desk and top drawer items

Nail varnish, cuddly little toy, greetings card, fluffy springy computer novelty thing that is suckered to the terminal, lots of different coiour pens, Hello! magazine, make-up bag, lots of perfume, spare pair of tights, spare pair of knickers, spare pair of shoes.

BIMBO

GOSSIPER

OFFICE MOTTO:
Plagiarism saves time.

GOSSIPER

Why the name?
Gossiper … Someone who frequently goes out of their way to cause problems, deliberately stirring up feelings or interest for (or usually against) something or someone, mostly out of petty jealousy because other people have lives and s/he doesn't.

How to identify type
Usually has wooden spoon somewhere on or near their desk.

Typical jobs
Secretary, Assistant (any kind), Post-Room Clerk, Dogsbody.

Names

Elizabeth, Nigel, Neville, Norman,
Mavis, Darlene, Marlene, Carleen,
Arlene, Leslie, Clare, Colin, Ian.

Dress code

Tries. But never succeeds. Buys from
all the 'in' shops of the moment,
but always gets it wrong.

Mannerisms

Swivel-heading (looking around them so
quickly it seems their head it swivelling a
full 360 degrees), ears flapping (listening
out for footsteps), foot shuffling (not

standing still so that if surprised they can appear to be in motion already).

Favourite sayings

- *Ooh-er, well I never!*
- *And what did he say then?*
- *Do you think he meant to do that?*
- *You'll never guess where he stuck his hand!*

Meeting Manners

Never allowed inside a board meeting room. The fallout would be catastrophic.

Chat-up lines

- *Let's go to my place and do the things I'll tell everyone we did anyway.*

Lunches
Sandwiches at desk, so they
don't miss anything.

Conversation topics
Other people.

Literature – books and papers
Heat, Hello!, OK!, Tatler, Cosmo, etc.

Hobbies
TV watching. Encouraging colleagues
to confide their innermost secrets
whilst telling them nothing in return.

Desk and top drawer items
Hello! and Heat magazines.

Things You'd Love to Say to Morons at Work

And your cry-baby whingy-arsed opinion would be…?

Do I look like a people person?

Sarcasm is just one more service we offer.

You?! Get off my planet.

Allow me to introduce my selves.

Did the aliens forget to remove your anal probe?

Whatever kind of look you were going for, you missed.

I'm trying to imagine you with a personality.

Too many freaks, not enough circuses.

Nice perfume. Must you marinate in it?

How do I set a laser printer to stun?

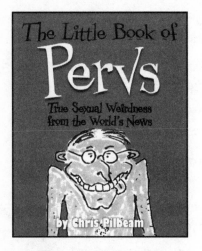

The Little Book of

Pervs

True Sexual Weirdness
from the World's News

by Chris Pilbeam

ISBN 1-905102-38-0
£2.99